Cottle Street

CONTENTS

CHAPTER ONE

Cottle Street is the worst street in town. Probably in the universe. And now Mrs Beam wants us to make it the most environmentally friendly one.

"She's stupid!"

"I like Mrs Beam," says Andrea.

"Yeah. So do I. Normally."

We walk in silence. Mrs Beam is our teacher. Usually she's great, full of fantastic ideas, new ideas. Usually she has the best ideas in the whole world. But this one? It's just too dumb for words.

"We could plant some trees," says Andrea, two paces behind me, sniffling as if she has a cold.

I give a scornful laugh. "What! Get real."

Andrea is my worst friend. She likes me no matter what I do, or what I say. She looks a bit like a mouse. She has pale brown, short hair, pale brown eyes, and she's only about half the size of an average nine-year-old.

Not that I can rave about my looks. My fair hair is always all over the place. And my blue eyes are too soppy for words. They are more like girls' eyes than boys' eyes. But at least I've got a good bowling arm for cricket.

"What about planting some flowers?"

"Yeah. And we could wash the footpath, as well." If it weren't for Andrea, I'm sure Sophie Paterson would be my girlfriend. Sophie and Sam. It sounds right. Instead, I've got Andrea, who follows me all the time, snorting and snivelling like a pig. Although, I don't suppose it's her fault she's got something wrong with her nose.

"Wait up, you two."

We stop and turn. It's Elliot. He lives above the shop on the corner of Cottle Street. His parents own it and the house next door. They rent the house to Old Archie Brown, who used to be a train driver when he was young. The shop is nothing like a supermarket. It's small and dark, but it's got the best pies. Elliot's in our class as well. I put up with him because he's got an endless supply of sweets and liquorice straps.

"What do you think?" he says, catching up. His round face is red from running. He pushes his dark hair out of his eyes.

"What about?"

"About the school's environmentally friendly street competition?"

"Sick," I say.

Andrea says, "I think it's a nice idea."

Nice? Andrea's got more wrong with her than I thought. We cross the railway tracks to Cottle Street.

"This calls for a special emergency meeting of The Club," says Elliot, dropping his voice to a whisper.

"What are you whispering for? There's no one around."

Elliot wants to be a famous detective when he grows up. He is always sneaking up behind people, hoping he'll find out something suspicious, but so far he never has. He narrows his grey eyes and glances around furtively, like a greyhound. "Bet I know something you don't."

We stop walking.

"If it's about Mrs Doon having a baby..." I say.

Elliot shakes his head. "Nope."

"Your pilot uncle is coming to stay with you?" says Andrea.

"He can't. He's in Africa."

I'm not sure about Elliot's uncle. He carries on about him, but nobody's ever seen him. Elliot says he can do all sorts of things in his plane. He says he's one of the famous Flying Red Hawks.

"Do you give up?" says Elliot.

Andrea nods. I don't like giving in to Elliot. "Sam?"

"OK," I growl. Who cares what he knows? It's probably nothing anyway. I start to walk up the street.

"It's Larry T.," says Elliot, keeping his voice low and secretive.

I stop in my tracks. "Who?"

"Archie Brown's grandson," pipes in Andrea.

Elliot frowns. "Hey! I'm telling."

"What about him?" I ask, wondering how come I'm the last to find out.

"He's come to live with Archie. He's..." Elliot pauses dramatically, waits for a second, then spells out the word, "B–A–D."

I shiver and look around. I feel secret eyes watching me, hiding behind corners. "So, what's this Larry T. done?" I ask. Now I'm whispering as well.

"Dunno. Yet."

Andrea looks very seriously at Elliot. "He keeps running away."

Elliot frowns at her. "And the rest," he scoffs.

"How old is he?" I ask.

"Fourteen," replies Elliot quickly, before Andrea can get a word in.

Andrea gives a long sniff. "Running away isn't all that bad."

"Uh uh!" Elliot shakes his head, and lowers his voice again. "Dad said he does other things. Really bad things." He takes a deep breath and stares at us.

"Like what?"

Elliot lets out his breath and shrugs. "I can't tell you now. I've got to go. I've got flute practice."

"I thought we were supposed to be arranging a meeting."

Sometimes Elliot makes me really mad. He's always trying to be like a detective. He likes having secrets and keeping things to himself. He probably thinks it's smart. But it's just stupid.

Andrea smiles. "It would be good if we could make Cottle Street the most environmentally friendly street in the whole competition."

"Yeah," I say out loud. While inside I'm thinking, dream on.

"Hurry up," says Elliot. "What time shall we have the meeting?" He holds up his arm so we can see his new watch. Elliot's parents give him everything he wants. Mum says it's not good for him. I wish I could get everything I wanted. Just to see what it was like. But that's almost the same as wishing Dad would find a job.

"Ohhh," says Andrea. "It's lovely."

I pretend not to notice. Although, it's hard when the digital, futuristic contraption is almost level with my eyeballs. What I would give for one of those! But Mum says money doesn't grow on trees. I know that. So why does she keep on telling me?

"How about tomorrow at four o'clock?"

Andrea looks doubtful. "I might have to look after Linda."

"Bring her," says Elliot.

I glare at him. Why did he have to say that? Last time Linda came to one of our meetings, she nearly wrecked the clubhouse. Only three years old, but boy can she motor. We spent most of the time chasing after her. She thought it was a game.

"Will that be OK with you, Sam?" asks Andrea, turning to me.

I nod. "Yeah." What else can I say? I don't want to be mean, just because Linda ruined our last serious discussion. We were going to make a video about a haunted house and sell it to a television studio for thousands. I'd written this really neat story. It was about an eagle who saved two children from a headless monster. Scary stuff. But we couldn't come up with a video camera. Not even Elliot. So we had to forget about it.

"OK. Four it is."

"And don't be late," I add.

Elliot comes to a standstill outside the shop. A notice hangs in the middle of the door that reads:

I've told Elliot it'd be better if the last line rhymed with the others. I've even written down suggested endings like "...ready on the dot" or "...nothing that will rot", but Elliot's only given me strange looks. He said his parents don't care about things rhyming.

After Elliot's gone inside, Andrea and I carry on down the street. I'm thinking about Larry T. What could he have done that was so bad? Fourteen's not so old. Perhaps he'd stolen a car? Or maybe...? No. I push the awful thought from my mind. But it comes back. In big, block letters. MAYBE HE MURDERED SOMEONE? I shudder. A murderer living in Cottle Street!

Andrea interrupts my wild thoughts. "It's a good prize," she chats.

"What?" I haven't a clue what on earth she's talking about.

"I'd love to see the penguins." She sighs and sniffs.

"Oh, you mean the competition." I switch my thinking back to the environmentally friendly street stuff. "Yeah. It is, isn't it?" I have to admit she's right. I'd give anything to see the penguins down the coast at Ryewater, then explore the rock pools, cook fish over an open fire on the beach, and sleep in the hut. "It'd be great."

"At least," says Andrea, "there're only two classes in it."

"That's still a lot of streets. And most of them have got flowers and stuff like that."

"Mrs Beam said being environmentally friendly doesn't just mean having those things."

"I know that. But look at this dump."

We both walk slowly in silence, staring at the street. The houses are old and wooden. The paint is flaking off them, and they look like half-peeled potatoes. Until today, I liked Cottle Street. I used to think it was a good place to live. Now I'm not sure.

Andrea stops outside her place. "You'll think of something, Sam. I know you will." She smiles trustingly at me. Then she goes inside.

See what I mean about Andrea? She can't leave me alone. She always reckons I've got the answers.

I trudge up the street, not knowing what to do. How does she expect me to come up with something when the last half of Cottle Street is taken up with Flynn's Car-Wreckers Yard?

CHAPTER TWO

Mum told me that once Cottle Street used to be OK. Years ago, before they built lots of shops down the other end of town. Now this part of town is mostly warehouses and factories.

On the corner of Cottle Street is the shop where Elliot lives. Next to the shop is a narrow alley. Then comes Archie Brown's house. Beside that is Andrea's house. Then there's a garage that's half falling down. Last is our place – it's two storeyed. Mum and Dad only rent it. I've never seen the person who owns it. Between us and the car-wreckers yard is a lumpy section of grass. There used to be a couple of houses there, but they were pulled down. It's overgrown and wild, but good for playing and practising my cricket. At the back of the street is the old railway station. It hasn't been used for years.

As I dawdle down the street, I get an idea. Imagine promoting Cottle Street as the most environmentally unfriendly street in the entire universe! Boy, that would surely be something different, all right.

By the time I walk into the kitchen, my head's crowded with images of thousands of people wanting to see Cottle Street.

Mum is sitting at the kitchen table. "Hi, dear." She shuffles something under a pile of papers. I know it will be a lottery ticket. *Win-a-Million – One scratch could make you a fortune*. The trouble is, Mum is spending a fortune buying the tickets.

"Hi, Mum," I say, pretending that I haven't noticed anything.

Once she won something. Way back in the beginning when the tickets first came out. I think it was $20. But ever since then, it's been a big, fat zero.

"How was school?" she asks, nodding and absent-mindedly pulling on her hoop earring.

"OK." I dump my backpack on the floor.

"Sam, don't leave it there." Mum lets go of her earring. She picks up an envelope and winds it into her ancient typewriter. She does the accounts for old Harry Flynn. He's the car wrecker. He's as rich as rich can be, but really mean and stingy. He hardly pays Mum anything at all.

"What's to eat?" I ask, banging the fridge door closed. As usual, there's only leftovers.

At the sound of my voice, Dandelion wakes up. She blinks her green eyes, yawns, and stretches. She's the fluffiest cat I've ever seen. When she walks, she seems to float just above the ground. That's why I named her Dandelion. She's pale orange and white. I found her two years ago, dumped at the railway station.

"I've made some muffins. I've put them away in the cupboard."

I go to the cupboard and take out two. I spread them with lots of butter and strawberry jam, then sink my teeth into one of them. "Yum. We've got this competition," I say, before starting on the second muffin. I lick the jam off my fingers.

"Sounds interesting." Bang, clank, clank go the keys on Mum's beat-up typewriter. "What's it about?" Clank. Clank.

"Having the most environmentally friendly street." I swallow the last chunk of muffin. "By next week."

Mum looks up from the typewriter. "What! Cottle Street?"

"Mrs Beam wants everyone to enter."

"Oh, well..."

I pick up my backpack. "It's stupid," I say.

I go to my room, throw my gear in one corner, and lie down on my bed. I think about Sophie Paterson's street. Trees and grass and neat things like that. Once, centuries ago, I went to her place for a birthday party. I think it must have been a mistake that I got invited.

I was the only boy. It was like going to another planet. I remember a big, pink birthday cake that had been bought from a shop. And stacks of wrapped presents. Unreal. Mum always makes my birthday cakes. Sometimes my presents as well.

I get up and walk over to the window. The room is stuffy and hot. I open the window and look out over a patch of grass, then across the tracks to the railway station. I sigh loudly. More than anything, I want to get to see the penguins. If only... I shake my head. It's no good. Nothing can put run-down Cottle Street on the map.

Sun streams over the deserted railway platform. At that moment, I see a movement. A shadow, skinny and long, dark and fleeting. I blink and duck down. My heart is pounding in my ears. What if it's Larry T., and he thinks I'm spying on him? A shudder runs down my back. Then, slowly, I lift my head until I can see the station. I sneak another look. But the shadow has gone.

CHAPTER THREE

"Linda, stop it."

Linda is pinging a small rubber ball, no bigger than a marble, against the inside of our clubhouse. The noise is driving me nuts. I'm trying to get organized for the meeting. Elliot's late as usual.

Our meeting-place is in old skinflint Flynn's yard. In one corner, he's got a pile of old car bodies. He reckons they're really good for collectors to buy and rebuild. I can't imagine it. They're total wipe-outs.

"Mum had to go to work. It's not my fault," says Andrea. Her mother often gets called to usher at the Majestic movie theatre in town.

"What's on?" I ask, eyeing the ball.

"Something about a strangled sausage."

"A what?"

Andrea gives a loud snort. "That's what it sounded like."

I shake my head. "It sounds really weird," I say. I can't imagine what she heard. The ball bounces in my direction. I grab it. Linda lets out a wail. It's louder than a police siren.

"Sam!" protests Andrea, giving Linda one of our club's biscuits. "He's only teasing."

"This is supposed to be a secret clubhouse for private members!" I yell. "I don't know why we bother." I sit and stew. I feel fed up. Mum scratched seven Win-a-Million tickets today. They were hidden in the rubbish bin. All duds. She thinks no one knows. I wish she'd stop.

Linda finishes the biscuit in one mouthful. Then she scrunches up her face, opens her mouth, and lets out another enormous wail.

"Give her back the ball," orders Andrea.

"OK, OK." I roll it along the floor. "But bounce it quietly," I threaten. "Or else." I pull one of my most frightening faces.

Linda giggles.

I scowl. "Where's Elliot? I've got to be home before dark."

Our secret clubhouse is an old ambulance. It has no wheels or anything, but it's got a big, empty space at the back. The back doors don't close too well. That's OK. We've got some good stuff inside: four pillows and one blanket; five puzzle books – all done (I gave those); a map of India; a pad of paper; two pencils; nine half-burnt, red candles (from Andrea's birthday cake); a roll of string; and lots of packets of reject biscuits. Elliot got those. His parents bought a whole box. They were supposed to be coconut and chocolate, but someone in the factory forgot the coconut.

I take a piece of paper and make a big heading: "How to Make Cottle Street More Environmentally Friendly".

I write with a green pencil. It's one I got from home. I'm making an effort to work with the environmental theme.

Next I write "One" and put a green circle around it. I'm just about to write "Two" when there are three raps on the door. Silence. Then another two. Silence. Then another one.

It's Elliot's secret code. No one uses it, except him. He says all decent detectives have one. He sticks his head around the half-open door. "I've got something to show you," he babbles, like he's all out of breath. Before he can say what, the door is yanked from his grasp and pulled wide open. The gap feels cold. Like when a tooth's gone.

Elliot stands grinning stupidly. Behind him is a tall, male figure, as skinny as a willow tree, with black hair cut very short, and eyes as dark as coal. He's wearing a pair of blue jeans, a T-shirt, and a black jacket.

I shudder. The stranger's shadow stretches across me. I know who it is, even before he speaks. Larry T., the Bad Larry T.

The next few minutes are a mess. All mangled up like a knotty nightmare. Bad Larry T. pushes Elliot aside. He reaches for the other door and flings it open. As the door hits the side of the van, the top rusty hinge rips off.

Now the door dangles, lopsided, from the bottom hinge.

"Hey!" I yell, flinging down my paper and pencil. I'm really mad. Who does he think he is? "Hey!" At that moment, I can't think of any other words. I stand up in a hurry. "Ouch," I gasp. My feet have got pins and needles. I sink back down.

Bad Larry T. springs into the van. He lands on his knees. He's as light as a cat after a bird. "Yeah? You talking to me?"

"Hey," I finish in a feeble voice. "Haven't I seen you before?"

Bad Larry T. begins to laugh out loud.

At that moment, Linda throws the rubber ball hard against the wall of the ambulance. It zaps about, hitting the wall, the roof, and the floor. Then it flies straight into Bad Larry T.'s laughing mouth, where it sticks in his throat.

In that instant, I know we're all doomed.

Bad Larry T. is turning blue in the face. His eyes stare at me. They look like they're going to pop out of his head. His face looks like a

crazed person's. Worse than anything I've ever seen on TV. He lunges at me, but slumps and falls. His head crashes sideways on the floor.

I jump up, then let out a scream. I'd forgotten about the pins and needles in my feet. "Ahhgh!" They hurt like anything. Too bad. I've got to do something. If Bad Larry T. dies, we'll probably all go to jail. But if Bad Larry T. lives, he'll probably kill us. Then he'll go to jail. I reckon that'd be better.

I bang him on the back, hard. Whack. Whack. Nothing. I bang him harder. WHACK. A gurgle. Much, much harder. THWACK.

The rubber ball pops out of Bad Larry T.'s mouth. Bad Larry T. coughs. I start praying.

Bad Larry T. lifts his head. The purple sunset is fading from his face, and his eyes have crawled back into their sockets. "Hey," he rasps.

"Linda didn't mean it," whispers Andrea. She swipes up the ball and stuffs it into her pocket.

Linda starts crying.

Elliot appears from around the side of the van. His face is white with fear.

"Hey, man," wheezes Bad Larry T. He lifts a skinny arm in my direction.

"I'm out of here," says Elliot. His voice sounds strange and hoarse, "I've got to go and practise my flute." He backs away, and disappears quickly.

I want to go home. Get out of the van, like Elliot. Some brave friend he is. Some great detective he's going to make. But I just can't bring myself to do it. Bad Larry T. is still half-slumped in the doorway.

"Does this mean the meeting's off?" says Andrea, still whispering. She quickly gives the whimpering Linda two more biscuits.

I nod. "Yeah. Tomorrow." The competition is the last thing on my mind at the moment. All I care about is getting out alive.

Bad Larry T. grabs my hand. "Hey, man, you saved me!" Slowly, he starts to rise. He's still tightly holding my hand. Crushing it.

"It was nothing," I say. Hoping he's not going to pulp my fingers. Cricket's coming up, and I want to try for captain this year.

"Nobody's ever done anything like that for me. Ever." He shakes my hand, then drops it.

I grin. A half-wrinkle, like a caterpillar on the move. "It's OK. Really. It was nothing."

Bad Larry T. pauses, his eyes narrow. "Don't tell me it was nothin'." His breath blows in my face. "You hear?"

I shrink back.

Andrea nods. "Last year, Sam saved me from being stung by a bee."

"Don't be stupid, Andrea," I growl. "He doesn't want to hear about that." Trust her to remember something like that now. "It wasn't anything special."

"It was so."

"I only stood on it."

Bad Larry T. cuts through our argument. "I owe you one." Then he turns, jumps from the back of the ambulance, and disappears down the darkening street.

CHAPTER FOUR

When I get home, Mum is sitting in the dining-room, knitting. She looks up and says, "Dad's just phoned."

Dad's working up north, on my uncle's strawberry farm. He hates it. Last time I spoke to him, he said he never wanted to see another strawberry in his life. I really miss him.

He used to work at the hospital, repairing the beds and wheelchairs. But, last year, they told him he wasn't needed any more. Since then, he's only been able to find casual work.

"What did he say?" I ask, sitting opposite Mum, watching her fast-moving fingers.

"He said he wished he was home."

Mum and I sit there silently. Both thinking to ourselves. Dandelion uncurls herself from the sofa, jumps down, and comes over. She nudges my knee, and I pick her up. "Yeah, I do, too." Mum doesn't say any more, she just keeps on knitting.

I eye the green thing she's making and hope desperately it's not for me. Mum's knitting is the pits. She never uses a pattern, just makes it up. Once, she made me a jersey. I couldn't wear it to school. It hung down to my knees like a dress. Mum said it would keep me warm.

I used to take it off and hide it in the garage, then put it on again when I got home from school. It was working well, until stupid Elliot saw me. He was on one of his detective missions. He said he wouldn't tell anyone, if I did his English homework for a week.

"What are you making?" I ask.

"I haven't decided yet." Mum pulls at the ball of wool tucked next to her. It's crinkly.

"It looks like it's been used already," I say.

"It's recycled wool," laughs Mum. "Turner's Thrift Bin had a whole container full of it in lots of different colours."

I shudder. That means she'll definitely be knitting forever.

Today is turning into a nightmare. First the environmentally friendly street competition. Then Larry T. nearly choking to death at my feet. And now Mum, with half a house of used wool, which she's going to be knitting into all sorts of things. Yuck!

That night, there's a thunderstorm. I'm in the middle of a weird dream when it wakes me up.

In my dream, Larry T. is sitting in the car-wreckers yard. He's knitting an orange snake. Elliot is sneaking around the place, taking photographs for evidence. Andrea and I are standing on the roof of my house, singing. Suddenly, the whole house starts shaking and rumbling.

"Hang on," I shout to Andrea.

She clutches my arm. Her eyes are like little rubber balls.

BOOM... BOOM... BOOM...

I look down. Now the whole of Cottle Street is moving and swaying sideways.

"The street," I scream. "I have to save the street. If I don't, it'll be recycled. Then Dad won't know where we are."

That's when I wake up. Thunder is crashing above me, my room feels like a boat on a wild sea, and I'm being tossed around. I'm just about to dive under my blankets, when Mum pushes open my door and comes in. "Are you OK?" Her hair is like a nest, and her face looks sleepy. "You were shouting."

I sit up. The room is very hot. "I must have been dreaming."

Another crash of thunder echoes above. The room shudders. I flinch and put my hands over my ears.

"How about some hot chocolate?"

I shake my head.

"Are you sure?"

I nod and yawn, pull up my covers, and lie down. Mum closes the door behind her.

Gradually, the thunder moves further and further away, until it is only a deep, faraway rumble. As I start to drift off to sleep, the stupidest thing comes into my head.

Recycle Cottle Street. Dumb. How can you recycle a whole street? Really dumb.

In the morning, I don't want to get up. All night, I kept dreaming and waking.

"Sam," Mum bellows from the bottom of the stairs. "Are you up?"

"Coming." I struggle out of bed, get dressed, and go down to the kitchen.

"I found this paper stuffed under the back door," says Mum, giving me a piece of paper, and two pieces of buttered toast.

It's a note from Elliot:

Dear Sam,
Got something important to tell you
about L.T.—
Meet me at 8:30
E.

I stuff the note into my pocket. I suppose the L.T. means Larry T. Elliot forgot to tell me where I'm supposed to meet him. Probably outside his place. I glance at the clock, it's nearly half past eight. I gobble down one slice of the cold toast, pick up my backpack, and head for the door.

"Hey!" calls Mum.

I stop.

"What about your lunch?"

I grin, and go back for it. "Thanks, Mum."

She bends down and kisses my cheek. She smells soft and warm like summer.

"I've got to go. See you."

I slam the front door behind me and race up the street. I wonder what Elliot's found out. If it's really horrible, I don't want to know.

Elliot's waiting for me outside the shop. He taps his new watch. "You're three minutes and fifty-two seconds late."

"What's so important?"

"Shush!" Elliot glances furtively down the street. "Keep your voice down."

We start to walk. The sun is warm on my back. Today is Friday, and every Friday afternoon Mrs Beam reads us an adventure story. I'd nearly forgotten about that with all the goings-on. The next minute, Elliot is whispering in my ear, interrupting my happy thoughts. "He was in on a bank job."

I gulp. My head buzzes. Cottle Street buzzes. Larry T. in on a bank robbery? A hold-up where they wear black things over their faces and carry shotguns?

I feel sick. "How d'you know?"

"I heard Dad and Archie talking last night."

Before Elliot can tell me any more, Andrea comes running up behind us. "Sam, wait for me."

Elliot scowls. "She really, really likes you."

"Don't be stupid."

"It's lucky she doesn't like me," says Elliot. "We detectives have to avoid things like that." His face turns pink.

When Andrea arrives, she gives a long snort of excitement. "Do you want to hear my idea for the competition?" she blurts. Her mousy-brown eyes twitch eagerly.

I nod, not taking much notice. I'm thinking more about bank robberies. And Larry T.

"Why don't we have a worm farm?"

Elliot and I stop in our tracks.

Andrea rushes on. "Worms are very environmentally friendly." She stops and looks at our blank faces. "Mrs Beam told us. Don't you remember? About how they turn all sorts of things into dirt."

I suppose Andrea's right. I mustn't have been listening at the time. "But what have the worms got to do with Cottle Street?" I ask.

"Do they have tractors?" jokes Elliot.

The happy look on Andrea's face wobbles. "I thought they could be part of the whole environmental thing."

I start giggling. In my head, I see hundreds of worms crawling up and down Cottle Street, being environmentally friendly. Smiling and waving to the crowds who have come to see them.

Andrea looks at me. Tears gather in the corners of her eyes. She screws up her little face and shouts, "I hate you, Sam Johnstone." Then she runs, as fast as she can, over the railway tracks, away from Elliot and me.

CHAPTER FIVE

Mrs Beam is nearly at the end of the adventure story, when an idea hits me about the environmentally friendly street competition. ZAP. In a flash, I know Andrea's right. Worms are the way to go. Cottle Street may be a dump. And it may be the worst street in the whole universe. But what does that matter?

My mind starts ticking over like a computer. Cottle Street is on the screen. I put in other information, like Mrs Beam saying that environmentally friendly doesn't just mean having green grass and flowers, then I add the worms, and Flynn's old cars. Finally, I press the computer button in my head, and wait to see what comes up. The screen goes blank, then... A BRIGHT BLUE FLASH.

Get Cottle Street to show lots of other environmentally friendly things, like Mum using recycled wool, Andrea's worms making dirt from scraps, even old Flynn's wrecked cars. Hey, yeah! Suddenly, getting to see the penguins seems possible.

"Sam," says Mrs Beam, interrupting my excited thoughts. "I asked you a question."

I snap out of my day-dream. I see the adventure book lying closed on her desk. She must have finished reading, and I didn't even notice. The rest of the class is staring at me.

"Sorry," I mumble.

"I was asking," says Mrs Beam patiently, "if you've thought of a theme for your street? For the competition?"

"Yes," I say, turning and grinning at Elliot and Andrea.

"Recycling."

At morning-break, Andrea rushes up to me. "I just knew you'd think of something, Sam," she says, forgetting for the moment that she hates me.

"It wasn't me," I say. "It was your worm idea that did it."

Andrea blinks. "But the recycling was all your plan."

Elliot creeps up behind us and taps me on the back.

I jump and swing around. "Don't do that," I shout. I'm not in the mood for Elliot to be trying out his spying techniques on me.

Elliot grins. "Good, eh?"

"No, it's stupid!"

Just then, Sophie Paterson and her friends walk past.

"Cottle Street needs recycling," she says, in a loud voice. The other two girls giggle.

"Dumping more like."

"Taking to the tip."

"Oh yeah?" I say. For the first time, I don't like Sophie at all. "Just you wait."

"What for?" smirks Sophie, wrinkling her nose, as if I smell. "The street to fall down?"

Now she's done it. Now I'm really mad. And without thinking, I blurt out, "Cottle Street's going to win!"

"What?"

"And my mother's the queen!" says the short, dark-haired girl. The three of them go off, twittering.

"What did you tell them we're going to win for?" asks Elliot. "Now we're going to look really dumb when we don't."

Andrea pulls her thin shoulders back, gives a loud snort, and says, "If Sam says we're going to win, then we are."

After school, I've got to go and have my hair cut. Mum told me she'd wait outside the school gates for me. But there's no way I'm going to let the other kids see Mum taking me to the hairdresser. So, while I'm waiting for

Sophie and her friends to leave, I go to the library, and hang around.

Ms Birch, the librarian, gets suspicious when I keep looking out the window, instead of at the books.

"Sam, do you want to get a book or not?"

I see Sophie and her friends walking in the direction of the library. I back away from the window. "I want some books on recycling," I say frantically, while thinking, don't let them come in here. Please.

I follow Ms Birch to the far corner of the library. All the time waiting for the library door to open but, thankfully, it doesn't happen.

"Here we are," says Ms Birch. She smiles, and runs her finger along the shelf.

Ms Birch is nice. She has pretty eyes, and the longest eyelashes I've ever seen. She pulls out a thin book. "For a project?"

I nod.

"How about this one on recycling paper?"

"That'd be good." I grin to myself. I hadn't even thought about paper. And there are probably hundreds of other things that could be recycled as well. I'll show Sophie Paterson whose street's the best.

By the time I leave the library, I can hardly carry all the books I've taken out. I see Mum waiting at the school gate, looking around for me anxiously.

"Sam, I was getting worried." She glances at the pile of books. "Well, there's no need to ask where you've been."

"They're to help me with ideas for the environmentally friendly street competition."

On the way to the hairdresser, I tell Mum my plan for Cottle Street.

She laughs. "It's a great idea," she says. "It's a pity Dad's not here. He'd have loved to have helped you."

As we cross the road, Mum says, "Oh, I nearly forgot. You had a visitor."

"Me? Who?" I ask.

"Archie Brown's grandson."

CHAPTER SIX

On the way home from the hairdresser, I tell Mum I've got to go and see Elliot.

"Not for too long," she says, taking the library books from me. "I'm going to start making dinner."

I make a beeline for the shop. I've decided to give Elliot his first real detective case. I'm going to hire him as my private bodyguard for as long as Larry T. is living in Cottle Street.

When I go into the shop, Elliot's father is leaning on the counter. He's reading the evening paper. He looks at me over the top of his glasses. "Yes, Sam?"

"Is Elliot in?" I ask. Mr Reynolds is OK. Mum says he's lazy, and it's really Mrs Reynolds who keeps the shop going. But he's always nice to me. He fishes around under the counter for a second, winks, then throws me a couple of packets of bubble gum.

At that moment, a hideous noise starts upstairs. It sounds like something's being killed.

"He's up there," says Mr Reynolds, raising his eyes to the ceiling. "Murdering his flute, and my ears."

I grin, go through to the back of the shop, and up the stairs. Mrs Reynolds is nowhere in sight. I bang on Elliot's door and push it open.

When Elliot sees me, he flings his flute onto his bed. "I wish Mum'd let me learn the guitar," he says, his face reddening.

"I've got a job for you," I say.

"Really?" His eyes light up. Then he frowns and looks at me suspiciously. "Who for?"

"Me."

"You? What for?"

"I need a bodyguard."

Elliot asks no questions and doesn't laugh. He nods, then walks, all important like, around his bed to a small table with three drawers down one side. "Don't look," he instructs.

I turn away. But in the mirror that's in front of me, I see Elliot bend over the table and fish a key from a secret hiding-place at the back. He opens the top drawer. "Can I look now?" I ask, pretending I haven't seen a thing.

"Hang on."

He pulls out a notebook, then shuts the drawer very quietly. "OK. Now you can turn around." He sits on the bed. I plonk down beside him.

I wait while Elliot writes in the notebook: C/1: B.G. – S.J.

"What does all that mean?" I say, looking over his shoulder.

"I can't tell you. It's highly confidential case coding."

At least he's better at this than playing the flute.

"OK," says Elliot. "What do you need a bodyguard for?" The pen hovers over the page.

"To guard me. What else?"

Elliot ignores my silly comment. "Why?" he asks sternly.

I tell him about Larry T. turning up at my place and asking for me.

At the mention of Larry T.'s name, Elliot starts to shake like a jelly. His face stiffens, and his eyes, nose, and mouth go all small and strangled looking, a bit like a squeezed lemon. "What'd he want?" he squeaks.

"I don't know." I shrug. "Do you want the job or not?"

Elliot shivers and glances around his room. "It's going to cost you."

"How much?" I hadn't thought about having to pay. I thought Elliot would be glad to have a case to work on.

"Five dollars a week."

I shake my head. I know what Elliot's up to. He's telling me I have to pay an expensive charge in the hope that I'll drop the whole idea. Then he won't look like a coward. I play along. "Get real. Where am I going to get that sort of money? Three dollars."

Elliot shakes his head and smiles a safe, satisfied smile. "Five dollars a week, or I don't do it. Danger money, you know. This is really heavy stuff."

"OK. You win," I say. "Five dollars a week." I haven't a clue where the money will come from. Maybe Mum will win something in the Win-a-Million lottery. But I have to say yes. I don't want Larry T. catching up with me when I'm on my own. "If I live, I'll pay you," I tell Elliot. "If I don't, then I'll owe you."

Elliot mutters something to himself and writes a few more things in the notebook. When he's finished, he hands me the pen. "Sign," he instructs, and points to a row of black dots.

I sign my name with a flourish.

Sam Johnstone

I stand up. "OK, now you can escort me back home."

"What? Now?"

"Yep," I reply. "Real detectives work all day and all night."

"But what about my flute practice?" protests Elliot.

I don't bother to reply. I open the door. "And real detectives always go first to protect their clients."

"But... um... but..."

"So...?"

Elliot drops the pen and notebook onto his bed. He shuffles past me, and I follow. We sneak down the stairs, tiptoe to the back door, then dart outside to the corner of the shop. After giving Cottle Street a good eyeballing from end to end, Elliot creeps out the gate. I follow his timid footsteps.

It takes us eighteen minutes to get home. Two houses away. Can you believe it? Elliot goes all around the block, just so we don't have to go past Archie Brown's house.

Mum's mad at me.

"Where've you been? I told you I was getting dinner."

"Sorry, Mum. I was discussing things with Elliot." I try to make it sound important. I look around for Dandelion, but she's not in her usual chair.

"I suppose it was about this environmentally friendly street competition?" she questions, as she points to me to sit down at the table.

I nod, telling myself it's not really a lie. In a way she's right. I was arranging protection for myself from being recycled in Cottle Street by Larry T.

"Where's Dandelion?"

"Oh, she's around somewhere."

A worry niggles at me. Dandelion always comes to say hello. Then I remember I didn't see her this morning. "Have you seen her around today?"

"Sam, stop fretting." Mum goes to the oven, gets out my meal, and puts it down in front of me without a word. Picking up her knitting, she sits in the chair by the window.

I know that mood. She's totally fed up with everything. Dad not being here. Her Win-a-Million tickets not winning a thing. And her knitting going all wrong.

I eat my dinner in silence. The vegetables taste like rubber, and the meat is dry. But I don't make a fuss, and I daren't not eat it, not with the mood Mum is in. Also, I know Mum's eagle eyes are watching me, even though she's knitting flat out. She worries that I'm not getting enough food. I swallow the last mouthful, gulp down the glass of milk, and am getting up from the table, when there's loud knocking at the front door.

I freeze. What if Larry T. has come for me? Where's Elliot when I need him? Especially now that I'm paying him five dollars a week, which I haven't even got.

Mum grunts and rips off a whole pile of stitches. "Sam, what are you waiting for? Get the door, before they bang it down."

I walk down the hallway. Really slowly. There's no way I can see who it is until I open the door. If only we had a front room with big windows. That way, I could sneak a look. Better still, if I could do karate. Then I'd open the door, give a wild cry, and fling myself into the air, like they do on the TV programmes. That way, I'd land on top of Larry T. before he knew what hit him.

"Sam," bellows Mum, after another round of knocking.

I open the door a crack, and peer around. When I see it's Archie Brown, and not Larry T., I nearly faint with relief. I swing the door open wide.

"Have you seen him?" asks Archie. He's a short man with fierce hair that sticks out like a bush. He has a fat red nose, sharp blue eyes, and no neck. He looks like a bullfrog.

I know who he's talking about. I shake my head.

"Sam, who is it?" calls Mum.

Archie brushes past me and marches up the hall, muttering to himself. I follow him into the kitchen.

"I said I would be responsible for him," grumbles Archie. "Now he's disappeared. And pinched my ladder."

"Your grandson?" asks Mum.

Archie sinks down into a chair, and puts his head in his hands. "Who else? Nothing but trouble since the day he was born."

I gulp. Perhaps he's gone to do another bank job? He'd probably need a ladder for that. Then the police will end up in Cottle Street. And it would get in all the papers: "Cottle Street Shoot-Out – Dangerous Bank Robber on the Loose".

Already I can hear Sophie Paterson and her friends rubbing it in even more about Cottle Street. So much for me shooting my mouth off about us winning the environmentally friendly competition. Not unless it's possible to recycle Larry T. from bad to good.

Mum waves her hand at me. She wants me to go away and leave them alone. But I can't move. It's like I've been stuck to the spot.

Out of the window, I've just seen the strangest thing in my whole life.

CHAPTER SEVEN

There, on the roof of the old railway station, is a figure creeping through the dusk like a cat burglar. At the far end of the roof is Dandelion. I'd know that long, fluffy tail anywhere, even in the half-dark.

"Look," I whisper.

"What...?" Mum shoots up from the chair and swings around. Her knitting falls in a pile around her feet.

Archie lifts his head and lets out a groan.

I'm out of the door like a shot. What if Larry T. frightens Dandelion, and she tries to jump? No, I won't think about it. Nothing's going to happen to her. I race down Cottle Street, running like I'm in the trials for the school's cricket team.

"Hey," I shout, as I pound up onto the deserted platform. I've got to warn him that Dandelion scratches like a tiger. She's OK with me, but she doesn't trust strangers, not after being abandoned. Larry T. pauses, looks down for a second, then decides to ignore me. I jump down onto the tracks in front of the railway station so I can see better. Larry T. is getting closer and closer to Dandelion.

Suddenly, Dandelion pounces with a hiss and a growl at Larry T.'s bare arm. The next minute, he lets a whole lot of words fly. Words I've never heard before. They fill the night like shooting stars. At the same time, Dandelion spits and hisses. Cottle Street fills with fireworks.

I clap my hands over my eyes. I can't look. I know they're both going to fall off the roof. I just know. And somehow it'll all be my fault. I open my fingers and take a quick peek. Both Larry T. and Dandelion are really going at it. Hissing, snarling, and screaming. Finally, there's one huge explosion from both of them. Then nothing.

I'm still too scared to look. I wait for the sound of bodies rolling off the roof. But it doesn't happen. I open one eye and squint up. I can't believe it. The roof is empty. I open my other eye and blink in the darkness. Then, around the side of the station, comes Larry T. clutching a wiggling Dandelion.

At the same time, Mum and Archie appear, both huffing and puffing like late trains into the station.

"I've warned you before..." bellows Archie, between breaths.

Larry T. ignores him and saunters over to me. "Is this yours, man?"

I nod. "How'd you..."

"I see things. And I owed you." He clicks his head back and pushes Dandelion at me.

"They'll put you away," rants Archie, rushing up to us.

"He's just saved my cat," I yell. Mum opens her mouth to tell me off for being rude, then closes it again. So, maybe I shouldn't have bellowed, but I don't care. Why does everyone think Larry T. is always up to no good? I take Dandelion and hold onto her tightly.

Larry T. spins away from us and starts to move off.

"Wait up," I call. Then I stop. Hey! What's wrong with me? What makes me think Larry T. is going to wait for me? One minute I'm scared to death of him. The next minute I'm trying to make friends. I'm really a case and a half!

At the sound of my anxious plea, Larry T. hesitates and stops.

I catch up to him. "She's never run away before," I babble. "It must have been all the thunder and lightning last night."

Larry T. walks silently beside me. His skinny head and body somehow remind me of the skull and crossbones on a pirate flag. We walk down the railway tracks, away from Cottle Street. There are no street-lights, just a big empty darkness.

"Sam, not too far," Mum calls out after me.

I swallow hard. I want to ask Larry T. if he really robbed a bank. But instead, I nuzzle my face into Dandelion's thick fur and say, "She was dumped."

"I had a cat," says Larry T., so softly I can hardly hear him.

"Yeah?" I say.

"Yeah." He cracks his knuckles. "He was totally black, with eyes like headlights, and really smart."

The railway tracks end outside a beat-up shed. Beyond that, there's nothing except factories and warehouses. We stop walking.

"He sounds a bit like Dandelion, except for his colour."

Larry T. smacks his fist into the palm of his hand. "Then one day – bang! He was run over. Gone. Just like my mum and dad."

A small breeze stirs the stillness of the night. Dandelion squirms in my arms, and I put her down. She stretches, then wanders back the way we came. I move after her. I'm not having her getting into any more trouble. "Do you want to come and see where Dandelion sleeps?" I ask, blurting out the first thing that comes into my head, trying to keep the conversation going. Trying to be his friend.

Larry T. doesn't move. He doesn't answer my question. He just stares out into the blackness. After a bit, he says, "See ya, kid."

I hesitate. I don't want to leave him standing all on his own in the middle of the night, in the middle of nowhere. But what can I do? "Yeah," I say. "See you." I move off after Dandelion.

And that's the last time I ever saw Bad Larry T.

CHAPTER EIGHT

The next morning, Mum is in a tizz. Dad's called to say he's got an interview for a job in a steel factory.

"If he gets it, we'd have to leave Cottle Street and move up north to live."

I stop pouring milk into my bowl of cereal. Leave Cottle Street? Never walk down it again? Never see Andrea or Elliot?

"Cottle Street's a rat-hole," smiles Mum, shaking her head. "But it's home."

All of a sudden, I'm crazy about Cottle Street. How can I leave it? In my mind it becomes a great, shining street with grand palaces. I'm in a big car driving along, waving. I don't know who I'm waving to, but I'm someone important.

"Well," says Mum briskly, picking up her huge lump of knitting. "We'd better wait and see what happens."

If we shift, I bet our next street won't have a railway station. Or a car-wreckers yard. Or my own cricket pitch. All at once, I feel like Larry T. standing on his own in the dark.

After I've finished my breakfast, I take the pile of library books, and go and sit in the bit of sun that's on the back doorstep. I've got to get things moving for the competition, seeing that it's next weekend. I write "Things That Can Be Recycled" on a piece of Mum's good writing paper, flick through the books, and start a list: "cardboard, newspapers, glass, bottles..." Dandelion comes over, nudges against me, and curls up at my feet.

I'm in the middle of writing "drink cans" when I hear a loud snort. It's Andrea. She appears around the side of the house, carrying a plastic ice-cream container full of dirt.

"Look." She holds it in front of my nose.

I peer at the lumps of earth. "What is it?"

"My worm farm."

"I can't see any worms." I start to snigger.

She snatches it away and screws up her face. "It's got three. So there."

She sounds like she's going to cry, so I quickly add, "It's great, really." At least Andrea's done more than Elliot and I have.

She looks at me suspiciously.

"Do you want to read about worm farms?" I rifle through the library books until I find the one I want, then the right chapter.

Andrea sits down beside me, still clutching the container. After a bit of reading, she lets out a long sigh. "Mine's no good. I need all sorts of things. And you can't see what's going on in it, either."

After a minute of hard thinking, I get an idea. "I've got it. How about using a jar? Or plastic would be even better. Then you'd be able to see everything."

Andrea gives an excited snort. "Mum's got heaps of empty plastic bottles out the back. Big juice ones."

"Hey, that's good. Worms recycling in recycled drink bottles."

Andrea smiles with pleasure. "I could make lots of them."

"It says here," I say, reading from the library book, "you've got to have some hay. Bits of old vegetables, newspaper, weeds, and manure."

"Where am I going to get all those things?"

I'm wondering exactly the same thing, when Elliot creeps around the corner. He's wearing dark glasses, and his hair is hidden under a wig made of silver paper. Last year, Elliot had to be an angel in the school play. Mrs Beam made him, as half the girls were away with chickenpox. That's where he got the wig. Luckily, I got to be one of the cows.

Elliot stumbles over Dandelion. Dandelion shoots up and hisses.

I glare at Elliot. "Watch out."

He stops creeping, and straightens himself up. He whips off the dark glasses and gives me a fast wink. "Coast's clear," he says, quickly putting on the glasses again.

"We need some manure," I say. I suppose I should really tell Elliot that I don't need his detective services any longer, but I can't be bothered explaining about what happened with Larry T. and me last night. At the moment, the competition is more important.

"And hay," adds Andrea.

Elliot sinks down onto the pile of library books. Dandelion waits until he's settled, then sits down well away from us, and starts cleaning herself.

"What's that?" asks Elliot, peering into Andrea's ice-cream container.

"Worms..."

"Look," I interrupt, "we need to get started."

But before we can make any plans, Mum comes to the back door. "Sam, your room is a disgrace. I want it tidied-up before we go to town." She gives Elliot a curious look, and vanishes inside again.

I throw down my paper and pencil, and jump up. I didn't even know we were going to town. How can I get things moving now?

Cottle Street might as well fall down. I stomp inside. "Well, what are you waiting for?" I shout to Andrea and Elliot. "Go and find some more worms."

Town isn't so bad, at least not until the sick chicken incident.

When Mum stops to pick up a couple of Win-a-Million tickets, I rush into a garden shop and ask if they have any hay. I'm going to explain about making a worm farm, but decide that no one would have a clue what I'm talking about. So instead, I say that I have a sick chicken. The shop assistant is really nice. She says they don't have any hay, but they do have some sawdust. Would that do? I don't have a clue if worms like sawdust, but guess it's better than nothing, so I say yes.

When the woman asks me what's wrong with the chicken, I make up a huge story about how it's losing all its feathers. And that's why

I need the hay, to keep it warm. I am just
getting into the middle of my sad story, when
guess who comes marching into the shop?
Mrs Beam!

Her round face lights up when she spots me.
She bustles over.

"Sam," she bellows, even though she's
practically standing on top of me. "Are you

collecting for your recycling?" Mrs Beam has the loudest voice in the universe.

The shop assistant is busy giving me two plastic bags full of sawdust. "Here we are. I hope your chicken is going to be all right."

"Err... yeah... thanks."

"Chicken?" bellows Mrs Beam. "You've got a chicken, Sam?"

I take the bags, and nod until I feel a bit like a puppet. Time to get out. Why did I have to go and invent the story about the chicken? Mrs Beam has got a thing about kids telling lies. Why couldn't I have just told them about the worm farm?

The shop assistant smiles at Mrs Beam. "What a nice boy. He found a chicken with hardly any feathers left on it lying on the roadside. How many kids would bother these days?"

Mrs Beam leans forward until her face is level with mine. She scans my face. "Sam?"

"It's very sick," I say to the floor, running out the door before she can question me. I bang straight into Mum.

"I've been looking all over for you."

"Sorry."

"Isn't that Mrs Beam?" Mum looks inside the shop doorway and waves.

"Mum," I wail, "come on."

"What's the rush? I thought you really liked Mrs Beam."

"I do," I mumble, already halfway around the corner. "Just not at the moment."

✻❖✻

Later that afternoon, Andrea and I are busy in the clubhouse, at last making some serious plans for the environmentally friendly street competition. Elliot's running late, as usual. He's probably taking the long way around, just in case Larry T. gets him.

"Is this OK, Sam?"

Andrea holds up a pile of signs labelled cardboard, paper, bottles, newspapers, jars, carpet, and clothes.

"What about cans?"

After she's written one for cans, she giggles. "What do you say we put up a sign outside old Flynn's yard?"

"That'd be a good one," I grin. The old skinflint will probably kill us. But too bad, it'll be over before he knows what's going on.

Andrea does a really large sign for recycled cars. As she's finishing off some twirly bits around the outside, Elliot bursts in through the door. He doesn't even use his own secret knocking code.

"Guess what?" he puffs.

"What?"

"He's coming."

Andrea's face goes pale. "Larry T.?"

"Nope. He's gone." He takes an important breath. "My uncle."

I grab Elliot's arm. "What do you mean he's gone?" I feel angry. I thought Larry T. liked me, and Dandelion. That we were sort of friends. I blink hard, as hot tears fill my eyes. I must be really dumb. He obviously couldn't have cared less.

Elliot shrugs off my hand. "Hey! I thought you'd be glad."

I let his arm go. "Course I am," I say, turning away.

"Don't say it's your uncle who flies the plane that's coming over?" says Andrea.

"Yep." Elliot glows at his brilliant piece of news.

Andrea and Elliot keep talking about it. They get all excited. But I can't. I can't stop thinking about Larry T. I can't stop thinking about him going off into the night, all on his own.

CHAPTER NINE

Suddenly, it's the morning of the competition. Saturday, a week later. But a lot has happened in between. The two biggest things are that Dad got a job in the steel factory, and Mum actually won $100 on a scratch ticket in the Win-a-Million lottery.

I've been really busy most of the week, collecting cardboard boxes for our recycled things, and writing out notices to let people know what we're doing. Then I got Ms Birch to photocopy them for me. She congratulated me and said it was a great project.

After school that same day, Elliot and I went to deliver the notices around the nearest warehouses and factories. I had to drag Elliot inside. But after the first one, he was OK. We gave them to people in the different offices. They all reckoned it was a good idea. One asked if we had a box for magazines and books. I said we did, even though we didn't. I decided we had better get one, fast.

Then we put the big boxes, with all their signs, in front of the houses right along Cottle Street. Elliot was in charge of the weather. If it rained, he had to get them all in. Andrea was busy collecting stinky vegetable scraps and leaves for her worm farms. "I'm going to sell them, as well as show them," she tells me.

I'm really envious. Andrea's quite clever. "Wow, you'll make a fortune," I say, wishing desperately that I'd thought of something so amazing.

Andrea gives a short snort, then smiles up at me. "The money is for the penguins."

Nobody knows about Mum and me leaving Cottle Street yet. I made Mum promise not to tell anyone until the competition is over.

In the whole week, there is only one sticky moment. That was when Andrea asked Mrs Beam where she could get some manure from.

A slow smile spreads across Mrs Beam's face. "Sam," she booms, so even the class next door can hear. "What about your chicken? Andrea could use some of its droppings."

Until then, I'd forgotten all about my whopping lie. My stomach sinks down, until it feels like it's hit the floor. Now I'll be in trouble. The last kid to lie in Mrs Beam's class had to write a whole page about why they had told the lie. An awful thought strikes me. Perhaps, instead, she'll ban me from the competition. Worse still, leave out Cottle Street altogether!

I pretend I'm flat out copying the sums from the whiteboard into my maths book. Thinking backwards and forwards, sideways, all over the inside of my head, for something to say.

"Sam?"

I know Andrea and Elliot are giving me strange looks, but at least they keep their mouths shut.

"It's dead," I mumble into my desk.

"Oh dear," bellows Mrs Beam. "How sad."

"Yes," I whisper.

At interval, Andrea and Elliot are down on me like a ton of bricks.

"You didn't tell us you had a chicken."

"Was it for the competition?"

I nod, working out in my mind that it was better to stick to my lie than tell the truth. Otherwise, it might get too complicated.

Cottle Street is being judged at ten-thirty. Mrs Beam and two others are coming. One is a teacher from Beacons High School, named Mr Stick. Mrs Beam told us he's a "greenie", whatever that is. She did explain, but I didn't take much notice. Something to do with keeping the world green, I think. The other is Mercy Marshall. She's the woman who writes about flower and vegetable gardens for the newspaper. I know the name because Mum is always saying, "Give me Mercy Marshall," when she's trying to grow some carrots and peas out the back.

I gaze down Cottle Street. It's looking really great. Most of the boxes are overflowing with stuff. The people from the factories and warehouses have been dumping things in them all week. The morning is hot. Already the sun is streaming in long ribbons over the old houses. Mum is sitting outside our front door, knitting. She's finally decided it's going to be a jersey for herself. It's now very long and full of wild, jumbled-up colours.

Elliot comes running down the street.

"They're coming," he puffs. It's been his job to be on lookout from his bedroom.

"Where's Andrea? She should be here."

"Dunno."

"Right," I instruct. "Have you got your flute ready?"

"Do I have to?" grumbles Elliot.

"Do you want to see the penguins?"

Elliot nods.

At that moment, Andrea appears. She is dressed up as a worm, all in brown. You can't even tell she's got arms and legs, they are all

wrapped up in old stockings. Over her head are two brown socks, joined together. There are two little holes cut out for her eyes. She wiggles up to us.

"That's great," I say.

"Wow," says Elliot, his mouth open wide.

Then I remember about the judges arriving.

"Quick," I say to Elliot. "Hurry."

I pick up my banner and run to where the street starts. The banner reads:

Welcome
Cottle Street is the name.
Recycling is the game.

The empty cans that I tied around the outside rattle. The newspaper streamers float in the breeze. Elliot trails behind. He collects his flute, and stands by his letter-box.

The judging committee arrive in Mrs Beam's car. Mrs Beam gets out first, then Mercy Marshall, and last of all Mr Stick. They are all carrying important looking clipboards and pens.

After Elliot has played *Happy Birthday* on his flute, there is a short silence until Mrs Beam claps. It's not really anyone's birthday, it's just that Elliot plays that tune best. The other two judges join in with the clapping, then hurry past.

They take ages. They look at everything, make notes, and stand around talking in whispers. They even ask Mum if she is part of it. Mum keeps a serious face and says she's knitting recycled wool.

Afterwards, Mum tells me Mercy Marshall asked her if she would make her something just like what she was knitting. She said she "absolutely must" have one. Mum said she had a hard time trying not to laugh.

By eleven o'clock, several people have turned up from the warehouses and factories to see how we are getting on. Cottle Street is getting full. Then horrors! Just as the judging committee is going towards the recycled cars, skinflint Flynn appears. He comes striding out from his yard. Trust our luck. We haven't seen him for days. I zip up to him.

"What in heaven's name is going on?" he asks. I step back. His breath smells like it needs recycling. I explain flat out.

"Humph!" He pulls on his pointy beard.

"Mercy Marshall's here from the newspaper," I tell him. Hoping he won't want to look bad in front of her, in case she writes something about him.

His small raisin eyes widen. "Well. Well."

It's nearly noon by the time the judges finally leave. They are half an hour late for Sophie Paterson's street.

Mr Flynn comes up and thanks us. That's a first. Usually he's bawling at us to get lost. He tells us Mr Stick wants to buy the old ambulance. It's just what he's been looking for. Andrea, Elliot, and I stare at him like idiots. I want to shout out that he can't have it. That it's our clubhouse. Then I remember that I won't be here much longer. Mr Flynn is busy telling Mum how Mr Stick is going to buy some land, do up the ambulance, then live in it and do "green" things.

"Oh, that reminds me, Harry," says Mum. "You'll have to find someone else to do your accounts." Then she tells him about us leaving Cottle Street.

Andrea looks at me for a second, bursts into tears, then turns and wriggles as fast as she can back up Cottle Street.

Elliot says sadly, "But now you won't see my uncle." He plods after Andrea.

Later, Mum comes up to my bedroom. I'm just lying there, staring at the ceiling, thinking about things. I don't understand why I feel so bad about leaving Cottle Street. Not long ago, I couldn't stand it.

Mum sits on the edge of my bed. "I'm really sorry Sam, for putting my foot in it before. I didn't mean to let the cat out of the bag."

I roll over and stare out the window. "That's OK," I say.

My bedroom feels safe and warm. The sun lies on the faded blue carpet, and the flowery curtains hang half over the long crack that runs down the window-pane. Through the glass, I can see the sky and the top of the railway station.

Mum speaks and breaks into my thoughts, bringing me straight back to what's happening. "Mrs Beam said something about a chicken. And how sorry she was it died."

I roll over onto my back and grin.

Mum shakes her head. "I can't imagine where she got such an idea."

EPILOGUE

Seeing the penguins was terrific. After Mrs Beam announced in front of the whole school that Cottle Street had won the environmentally friendly competition, Sophie Paterson told me she was never speaking to me again. I told her right back that she wouldn't be able to anyhow.

Mercy Marshall did half a page on us for the newspaper. Unreal. All about Cottle Street, the recycling stuff, and Andrea and her worm farms. Then she came and took photographs of us at the penguin colony. WOW!

Mum bought sixteen copies of the paper. She sent one off to Dad, and the rest off to the other relatives. And she's promised that during the holidays Andrea and Elliot can come and stay. Elliot told me that his uncle might fly them up. Andrea gave me one of her worm farms. So that's about it. Except for one other thing.

When I got home after the penguin weekend, Mum gave me a package. There was no stamp on it. As I ripped it open, I couldn't imagine who it was from. Out fell a brand-new cat's collar, black with a silver bell in the middle. The bell jingled as I lifted it out.

It had to be from Bad Larry T. Now Dandelion won't get lost again.

When Mum asked me, "Who's that from?" I answered, with a silly smile all over my face, "A friend."

FROM THE AUTHOR

*C*ottle Street is like the street I lived in when I was growing up. Most of the homes were old and run-down. And the kids from Cottle Street are a lot like the kids from my street. Because we didn't have much money, we had to make do with what little we had. We started a spy club and spent hours sneaking around behind hedges desperately hoping to discover something exciting. We never did, though!

But we invented things, made up plays, gave concerts, and played all sorts of games.

My mother always had ways to save money. She would unravel metres of wool to knit us "new" jerseys. A lot of our clothes were "hand-me-downs", recycled at least three times before the next child got to wear them!

When I think about it, *Cottle Street* is made up from a whole lot of little pieces of me. The kids, the lack of nice things in life, the making do with what we had, and – of course – the street itself. In a way, you could say I've recycled all those things into the story of *Cottle Street*.

ELIZABETH PULFORD

FROM THE ILLUSTRATOR

Recycling is an organized operation in our household. Everything that can be recycled goes into a big box. At the end of each month, when the box is overflowing, the whole family sorts out items for recycling.

This is an exacting affair, as my partner, Kim, and I are closely refereed by our 3-year-old daughter, Tessa. If we so much as look at the box of plastic bottles while holding a glass bottle, she'll point to the box containing the glass bottles.

I feel sad when I see how much rubbish we still throw away, knowing it could take years to break down.

I have been illustrating children's books since 1992, and I am proud to say that this is the second novel I have illustrated for Elizabeth Pulford. Elizabeth's characters and stories teach us that taking care of our environment requires us to make certain sacrifices and be more thoughtful. Knowing we are caring for our environment however is its own reward.

BRENT PUTZE

CONFIDENCE AND COURAGE

Imagine this, James Robert
Follow That Spy!
Who Will Look Out for Danny?
Fuzz and the Glass Eye
Bald Eagles
Cottle Street

SOMETHING STRANGE

My Father the Mad Professor
A Theft in Time: Timedetectors II
CD and the Giant Cat
Chocolate!
White Elephants and Yellow Jackets
Dream Boats

ANOTHER TIME, ANOTHER PLACE

Cloudcatcher
Flags
The Dinosaur Connection
Myth or Mystery?
Where Did the Maya Go?
The Journal: Dear Future II

WHEN THINGS GO WRONG

The Long Walk Home
The Trouble with Patrick
The Kids from Quiller's Bend
Laughter is the Best Medicine
Wild Horses
The Sunday Horse

Written by **Elizabeth Pulford**
Illustrated by **Brent Putze**
Edited by **Frances Bacon**
Designed by **Nicola Evans**

© 1997 Shortland Publications Inc.

09 08 07
11 10 9 8 7

Published in Australia and New Zealand by MIMOSA/McGraw-Hill,
8 Yarra Street, Hawthorn, Victoria 3122, Australia.
Published in the United Kingdom by Kingscourt/McGraw-Hill,
Shoppenhangers Road, Maidenhead, Berkshire SL6 2QL

Printed in China through Colorcraft Ltd., Hong Kong
ISBN 10: 0-7901-1689-8
ISBN 13: 978-0-7901-1689-1